The Diary of a Proper MRS

Rachel Coy

All rights reserved. No part of this publication may be reproduced, distributed, or transmitted in any form or by any means, including photocopying, recording, or other electronic or mechanical methods, without the prior written permission of the publisher, except in the case of brief quotations embodied in critical reviews and certain other noncommercial uses permitted by copyright law.

Copyright © Rachel Coy, 2022.

Table of contents

Chapter 1

Are you going to go without giving Kate her flakes first? John blasted my way.

I made my way to the door. John said, "Feed her yourself."

He gave me a look. "Have you ever taken on a motherly role? Always put your modeling career before raising a family! That dumb, awful modeling job!

I abruptly stopped and yelled at him. Is the reason for all of them only because I instructed you to feed kate?

"Who gave her food up till now? I'm rushing to go to work this morning; are you not meant to utilize your senses, even if you don't have any?

At him, I grinned. "You should feel glad that I'm still with you after this marriage's five dreadful years. Do you know the kind of males I encounter daily in my field? Even if there are better guys than you, I will continue to support your poor ass.

"Gloria, let's get divorced." He entered our room and came back with a white sheet and a pen. "I came prepared because I anticipated a day like this would occur. Sign".

I was astounded to see the guy who had revered me for five years being so ready to get rid of me. Without giving it a second thought, I signed the document, and I could instantly see relief in the idiot's eyes.

He held out his hand. "Well done, miss Johnson,"

Johnson was the name of my father.

The well-known Benedicta Martin, who had just divorced, was returning as Benedicta Johnson. Back to single life after married life. John was permanently departing my life.

I was still taken aback by his behavior. Are you not worried that you could lose the ever-famous celebrity?

He grinned. "Every true guy aspires to be married and a father. The guys who are crouching around you will flee once they discover who you are.

"I'll find a lover," the speaker predicts.

He laughed. I wish you success.

I hurried in to get my luggage and the suitcase for my infant.

When I went back to the sitting room, John was feeding kate.

At him, I clench my teeth. "I'm bringing kate with me."

He shrugged. "...if she permits you, however."

"Permit me? Who are you speaking to? I am her mother, and I bore her for nine months in my belly.

Is that sufficient for motherhood?

Have you ever taken on the role?

Or is all you do to lay eggs?"

I grabbed Kate away from him, but as soon as my infant was in my arms, she began to sob vehemently. She resisted being in my arms and retreated to her father's arm.

She refused to eat from my hand after I stole the food from him.

I gave John kate's dish of food, and he took it. She is aware of the maker of the flakes. She is aware of the effort's maker. She is aware of the flake maker.

I left the home with my luggage while leaving Kate's bag behind.

My daughter turned me down.

John was he right?

He was always in charge of producing the flakes.

He always put in the most effort.

I would never be able to return to Benedicta Martin, no matter how much I wanted to.

Or did it?

A young woman welcomed me and proceeded towards our home before I had even left the house.

I stopped her. What do you desire?

"I am great friends with John."

"What brought you here?"

“He is divorced now. I thus owe you no explanation.

"With John, I had a kid."

"Wow! I had the impression that Kate had no mothers.

She infuriated me. "Are you insane?"

"There's no need for you to spend time. John will never consider being married to you again, no matter what you do. He is very happy to have divorced you. When she touched me on the shoulder, I saw my kid rush up and enthusiastically embrace her.

My child.

I realized it.

This weird lady was going to take my house away.

John was engaged to be married.

I suddenly realized that I was going to lose both my kid and the guy I loved most dearly.

I had never been so afraid in my life.

My telephone rang.

It was my boss. I connected the connection reluctantly.

Hello Mrs. Benedicta Martin, Colyn Pampers would like to have you represent them in their next advertisement and...

"I am now a miss instead of a Mrs. Call me Benedicta , please. I told him.

Now that I think about it, once sponsors learn that I'm not hooked up anymore, I was going to get additional offers.

I was split between my desire to become the most renowned lady in the world and my dread of letting another woman take my house.

In addition to wanting to be the most well-known lady in the world, I also didn't want to lose my husband and kid.

I was going to advance in the field while refusing to let that lady rule over me in my own house. Benedicta Johnson, I understand you are now divorced. Who would have imagined that despite being the most honorable public person I have ever met, you lack the maturity to defend your home? When we ran into one another at Clarity Event Hall, where Coker Lee was enjoying his 30th birthday, the older sister of a prominent star who was a fan of mine responded.

I was unable to speak because I was so ashamed. I could hear murmurs as I continued to go. I had become a divorcee, and word had gotten out.

With each passing day, it seemed to hurt more.

I was shocked to see renowned Coker Lee leaning against my vehicle as I went to it.

My heart somewhat jumped.

I made a friendly wave. Hello, Coker Lee.

He unexpectedly approached me for a hug. "Benedicta , can we become friends? You were specifically brought here because I needed you to comply with my request.

I was astounded by his demand. "Me? to have a buddy like you?"

"Yes. Please grant my request if you can.

"Sure," you say.

He went happily back into the hallway after we exchanged contact information.

I had already been divorced for three weeks when I learned that I would soon become more well-known.

I want to be friends with Coker Lee!

When I got home that night from work, the tension in my family's home was still there.

Still, my parents refused to communicate with me.

They thought I was the worst kid in the world since I had divorced John without their consent.

All I had to speak to were my siblings.

In December, Debbie, the youngest of my siblings, will wed a struggling architect.

Up until that moment, I had believed that my siblings didn't object to my divorce.

He's still a very struggling architect, Debbie. Are you certain he'll be able to look after you? Being the eldest of the Johnson girls, I forewarned.

Debbie gave me a look.

She had never previously given me that kind of a look. "Do you remember those times when you and John were so much in love? John was making $50,000 per year, but you pushed the wedding and reminded us that finding the ideal spouse is not only about how much money someone makes. Look at you now, still acting like a miss. Never would I ask a divorcee for a marital counselor if I needed one. She hissed.

That stung.

I had to change my mind and leave my parents' place.

I was turned down because of what I did.

I needed to go.

I had to go to the grocery store later that evening with my third-born sister, Juliet, to replenish the fridge.

We proceeded to the Zonta grocery store, and as soon as I parked my vehicle and walked out, I saw John's car parked in the same spot.

John was at the grocery store.

As I entered with my sister, my heart started to beat more rapidly.

When we arrived at the grocery, Kate was making a scene.

That odd woman, who intended to kidnap my family, was chasing after her as she fled about.

My kid was seized and placed in my arms.

When I heard my kid murmur, "mummy," my heart skipped a beat. I was identified by my kid.

I was her mother, and she was aware of this.

My eyes were flooded with tears of excitement as I repeatedly embraced her.

John took her away from me and gave me a critical look. "I've heard you're seeing Coker Lee right now. Very well done. He muttered.

"I've heard that you're seeing that odd woman again. Very well done. I was furious when I saw him hand my child over to the strange woman.

I ran out, trying to collect my breath, without even buying what I wanted to.

From behind, I could hear stomping.

When we left the home, my sister did not wear heels, so I first believed it to be her.

I turned around and there she was—the odd woman.

She grinned and waved. Benedicta Johnson: "Hello."

She highlighted my father's name, which just made me despise her more.

So that Kate may have a larger playhouse, "We will be packing up from that home and moving to a nicer spot."

"We? Do you share a home with my husband?

She laughed. "Gloria Johnson, you don't have a spouse. I have been anticipating this day for seven years because I adore the guy you refer to as your spouse. Never again will I allow John to escape my control the way he did the first time.

Chapter 2

I fixed my gaze on the bathroom mirror while I used it.

DARK.

I was unable to see anybody.

John was the only one I could see.

when we first met. Before that fateful day, we had been seeing one other for quite some time.

Wednesday morning was chilly.

I can recall it just like yesterday.

Back in time.

I hurried into the drugstore.

My elbow had been aching since the morning when I accidentally banged it on the kitchen door, so I was seeking a pain reliever.

I was meant to take the medications that the pharmacists advised.

I rushed outside and attempted to block a cab.

Back then, I didn't have a vehicle.

Unexpectedly, a private vehicle stopped and offered to pick me up.

My parents would often send me terrifying real-life WhatsApp videos of young women being raped or killed, and I became afraid to accept lifts as a result.

I thus refused the lift offer, but as soon as he lowered his side window, I knew who he was! He was employed at the electricity firm that is in front of our home.

Every time I waited at the bus stop to be taken to my workplace, I invariably leaped into him.

The young man's place of employment at the electrical firm was just next to the bus stop.

I got into the vehicle, trusting the kind look he was giving me.

As he continued to drive, he offered me a glass of water while gazing at the medicine package I was holding.

That was the kindest thing a guy had ever done for me.

It feels very bad, right?"

I blinked. "Since morning, while I was attempting to acquire a spatula to stir the Egusi soup that was already on fire from below, I, uh, stuck my hand on the kitchen door. You must see how my elbow impacted the door so forcefully given the energy I used to get the spatula. Blood didn't spill out, but I had never experienced such agony.

He looked at my elbow. "Can I see the prescription medications?" He looked through the recommended medications, and then he immediately had me take each one in turn.

That evening, he drove me to the hospital.

He remained with me for three hours nonstop.

I had dozed asleep when I opened my eyes to see this weird figure standing vigil over me.

When I opened my eyes, the ache was gone entirely.

He quickly offered me dinner and drove me home.

It had started that way.

I experienced my first ever true love when John became my closest friend.

Because I believed in him, I didn't mind that his automobile always spent more time at the mechanic's shop than at his ranch.

The guy I cherished had promised.

Regardless of his used automobile, I saw John's potential.

Right, believing in someone was the act of loving them.

But did our unwavering love vanish in only five years?

The first guy I slept with was John.

I could still see how I had encircled him in an attempt to protect my closest buddy from being taken from me.

kate was nonetheless born.

And I have no idea what occurred because kate brought us the most joy we had ever had.

Were we so preoccupied with making it in life that we lost sight of how to maintain the fire, or did we just become weary?

Right now.

As soon as I left the restroom, my head started to hurt once again.

Steps were heard behind me.

It was my mother.

She drew me to the balcony while holding my hand.

What's wrong with you, I ask.

Do you wish to end your own life?

I cried and hopelessly hugged her. "Mom, I'm not sure what's going on anymore. I regret what I did. I want to return to John and my baby.

Yes, but you wouldn't because of your pride.

"Mum, do you believe I chose the wrong spouse?"

"No. You both lost concentration and signed documents like the dupes you are because you had been seeing too many American movies.

He was ready to let go of me, I could tell.

"... and if you make amends to your spouse, heaven will open its doors and let you in."

"John will return for me if he genuinely loves me,"

"Only a lady who has shown that she is ready to be a genuine woman can a real guy return for her."

"Never! I can never convince that moron of anything! Never".

"Then put everything behind you and continue! Proud to be a human! I was left on the balcony by her.

I was unable.

I couldn't only focus on improving myself for that church rat.

John, Kate is now dozing off. When are you planning to retire?

He gave his laptop a focused type. I'll do it later. Katie, I appreciate you putting kate to sleep. You may retire to bed. I'll go to bed later.

"Since your wife departed, you haven't stopped working."

He laughed. How many times do I need to tell you, Katie, that I no longer love that person? The worst wife there ever was, she

"Love is so unjust; sometimes we can't help but fall in love with someone who doesn't deserve it."

I'll never be able to return to that lady. Do you not realize that I cannot love such a person? You saw how much pain I endured at that woman's hands, and now you think I could love someone like that?

Will you accept that lady if she changes and comes back, John?

"That lady is unchangeable."

"My issue is, what if she changes tomorrow? If Benedicta Johnson resurfaces as Benedicta Martin, would you accept her?

John breathed out loud. "I will accept my wife even if she changes tomorrow."

Katie watched him as she choked. Then, John, why do you still have me in your life? "Why? Are you trying to assist me? Why do you think I'm assisting you with Kate, I ask. He shrugged. "Of course, as a good buddy. Good friends provide unintentional assistance. "John, why is it so difficult for you to think of getting married?"

I consider you to be nothing more than a buddy, Katie. I have no intention of using anybody, so if you're not OK with that, you must go.

Sadly, she sighed. No matter what you experienced at your wife's hands, I have faith that you will find love again.

I won't be getting married again, Katie. Look for better guys in the world today. Do not have any hope in me.

Katie breathed out loud. Hire a babysitter, then. If they don't see a future with me, I can't stay on as their nanny.

When I was informed that someone wanted to meet me in my office, I had just completed a commercial with the agency.

I was quite shocked to see Coker Lee there.

The moment I walked into the office, he hugged me. "Benedicta , how have you been?"

"Whoa! I was shocked to see you!

Yes, I'm here to request something vital from you.

"Important? Please speak with me.

Do you mind becoming my girlfriend?

My phone rang while I was considering Coker Lee's request outside in the garden.

It was my mother.

"Good day, mummy?"

"A notice board was in front of your husband's new home as I drove by. He wants to hire a babysitter. Your adversary seems to have left. Seize the chance, and look after your daughter the way you would want her to be looked after.

However, mom, are you certain that he won't believe that I'm doing all of this to get close to him?

rely on my mum.

She snapped the line off indignantly.

The sound of my beating heart could be heard louder than the knocks I was making on John's new house's large gate, however.

I followed the security guard's directions to the large home, where I sat down on a cushion that was handed to me and had a look around the disorganized living room.

littered playhouse, water on the floor, the stench of urine, and cornflakes.

I stood up as soon as I heard his footsteps.

When he saw me, he was stunned. "Benedicta ?".

"Good morning, sir. I come to submit my application for the position of nanny. I'm hoping you'll hire me, sir.

Chapter 3

"Benedicta ? What do you have to do here?

I breathed out, trying to suppress the feelings that were building within me. Hello, sir. I came to submit my application for the position of nanny. "Have you ever worked as a nanny?" He cooperated. "I am a parent. I was also an excellent mother. I said haughtily as I saw him hide his laughs. "Where is your kid right now?" At that time, Kate rushed to embrace me.

I exclaimed as I carried her. "My kid is here, right now."

"What gives you the impression that I'm going to hire you?"

"Why don't you give me a month to prove myself, and if I don't live up to your expectations, you can kick me out."

He gave a meaningful nod. "I only give you one month."

I need to shower her as she just got home from school.

I bathed her, creamed her, and dressed her.

her favorite black and yellow dress.

She still had her yellow ribbon in her drawer.

I fastened it to her hair while admiring my lovely kid.

As I watched her favorite show on television and swept the living room, I brought her over to the sofa and sat her down on the cushion.

To get rid of the pee odor, I spJohned an air freshener. When John left the room, I could see the surprise on his face.

I breathed out clearly. I'm through for the day. I pledge never to let you down. I left the home on foot.

I felt joyful in some way.

I was pursuing my greatest desire.

to look after kate.

A white Hummer Jeep had been stopped in front of my vehicle for over five minutes and was not moving as I made my way back home.

The fact that it was in my path prevented me from turning around since the route was too small.

When I jumped out of my vehicle to confront the driver, Coker Lee was there, too to my utmost surprise.

He stood in front of the Jeep Hummer and was extending a piece of cardboard at my face.

It had writing on it. Martin Benedicta , would you marry me?

My heart sank.

He had asked me to be his girlfriend only yesterday.

Now engaged?

It offered me a strong temptation.

Before I knew it, a sizable throng had formed around us.

include TV hosts with their on-camera recorders.

"Hrrrrr! Say "yes"! Just say yes! They pleaded.

My telephone rang.

It was my mother.

I plugged the line in. "What's going on? Do you accept Coker Lee's proposal? You didn't tell him that you still had feelings for your spouse, did you?

"I've had it with John,"

I felt a touch behind me.

I twisted.

John answered.

He had my purse in his hands. "You didn't have your purse," He mumbled.

When I saw him, my heart sank.

I had already informed my mother that I was over John, but if I marry Coker Lee, I won't have any chance at all with John.

I tell the truth.

I still loved this obstinate guy much more than I had previously believed.

Why did John have to show up just as I was ready to make the most difficult choice of my life?

He rolled his eyes as I looked into his eyes as if he didn't give a damn.

He handed my bag to me before leaving.

I turned to face Coker Lee and feigned a grin. "As you are aware, I just got divorced, and it hasn't even been a month. So why don't we start as friends so I can learn from the errors I made in my previous marriage? I tried to speak as nicely as I could. The people who were around us at the time could be heard having talks that were disappointing, but I stuck to my position.

I stepped over to hug him before returning to my vehicle and leaving.

I was the only one in the living room, sitting on the cushion.

I mentally relived the day's events in the dim living room.

From my nanny chores, which included washing my kid and gazing at John's troubled eyes, to Coker Lee's proposal scenario, everything was vivid.

Coming from the tunnel, I heard footsteps.

Dad was there.

I exhaled heavily. "Dad? What took place? unable to sleep?

On the cushion that I had curled up on, he took a seat. We saw your video. You declined the offer from that famous person. Why?". He quietly enquired.

I sighed. "I knew I couldn't do it when John arrived to give me my bag. Aside from John, I don't believe I can marry anybody.

You adore him.

I really can't marry someone else, even though I know he doesn't feel the same way.

Dad gave a meaningful nod. Your mother informed me that you are now his nanny, she said. Make a lasting impression on him and make him regret ever leaving someone like you. Be the ideal wife that any guy would want in his life.

I stepped into my office to collect my handbag after posing for Tone Creams photo shoots, but two of my coworkers barged in from behind.

"Hey! We have heard that you are now the husband's nanny. That is the most bizarre thing I've ever heard. What did you intend when you did that? That query came from the Queen, who glanced at me with trepidation.

I had this notion that they would inquire about Coker Lee.

They asked me a more challenging question instead of the Coker Lee proposal from yesterday.

Diana moved the Queen. "Are you certain she didn't submit her application to become a nanny because she missed her husband? Oh, how romantic. They started laughing and left my office right away.

I arrived at my ex-new husband's home the next morning.

When I came inside, he was still asleep.

He was lazily dozing off on the sofa.

John never fell asleep on the sofa unless he was beyond exhausted.

He had left his laptop on.

I fixed my gaze on the display.

He had done some study on Coker Lee.

I shrieked.

How long has he been looking up information on him?

He had been acting as if he didn't care, but in reality, he was so concerned about it that he had done so much study on it that he had even fallen asleep.

I went to his room and got a cushion for him.

Before I could turn away from him after putting his head on the pillow, I felt his arm around my waist.

In the process of putting the pillow under his head, I accidentally roused him, and now he was stroking me softly and reminding me of those wonderful times that I didn't want to recall.

You arrived so early, He muttered.

"Er...yes". I hesitated.

Why didn't you arrive yesterday, I asked.

"Work suddenly summoned me for a Tones Cream photo shoot. I contacted you, but it seems that you banned my number, most likely after the divorce.

He gave me a serious nod before gently letting go. I'm sorry about how I touched you earlier. You being here so early surprised me, so I

I gave a serious nod. "No issue, sir. I grabbed the cushion since I saw how exhausted you looked and wanted to prevent your neck from hurting too much when you woke up.

"Not at all an issue." His tone was quite cold.

He didn't want to speak about it at all, so he touched me about the waist and placed a pillow under his head.

He stood up and picked up his laptop from the sofa where he had left it. When he realized it was still on, he exclaimed. "Have you searched the laptop?"

I sighed. "I believe that since the laptop was already running when I came, I just didn't stop my eyes from performing a few things."

It was clear that he felt ashamed. "I wanted to know why Coker Lee suddenly became so interested in you, and I did find out the cause."

I was puzzled. He didn't do it because he liked me,

He gave a headshake. "I faced up against a rival in both high school and college. We constantly engaged in competition in school, sports, and with Joan. The now deceased Joan liked me a lot, but my rival adored her.

You didn't adore Joan, right?

"I did it because she loved me so much, but my rival loved her much more. But one day, when I was having a conversation with my friends at the pool party that our department had planned for the weekend, she drowned. He was ill, therefore he had decided not to attend the pool party. We were then in the third year of college. Since then, he has held me responsible for Joan's passing and has threatened to one day make me experience the same pain he had as a result of Joan's passing. Coker Lee wants you because he believes that I feel the same way about you as he did about Joan. Coker

Lee thinks that you are the one that I love most in the whole world, thus he would stop at nothing to get married to you.

It was logical.

Coker Lee's surprise proposal and want to be my buddy.

He did all he could to harm John.

My telephone rang.

It was Coker Lee.

Discuss the devil.

I set the speakers on and connected the line.

Greetings, Coker.

Whereabouts are you?

He seemed to be aware of my whereabouts.

"I arrived at work."

"You're not working. You are now in your former husband's shoes. How are you using the place? Was it the reason you turned down my offer two days ago? From now on, cease becoming your husband's babysitter. Do you understand?"

"But what if I don't?"

"I couldn't care less if you didn't! I am aware that you work there because you adore him. I am aware that you rejected my offer because you adore him. I'll use every force at my disposal to win you over to my side. Everything!!!".

John was accurate.

Coker Lee was fixated on me because he still considers John to be his biggest rival.

Chapter 4

My life had an upsetting occurrence the next morning.

Katie was back at home with my spouse. the unusual lady. She gave me a look. I didn't believe it when you told me you were Kate's nanny until I arrived to verify it. I gave her a kind grin. Of course, a forced grin. I don't have the authority to look after my kid, do I?" She shrugged. You can be Kate's nanny, but you'll err if you attempt to be John's nanny instead.

"I don't need to talk to my ex,"

I'll be residing here going forward.

Yes, but I want to make it clear that you are not my employer, so please refrain from directing my actions. To get Kate ready for school, I headed to her room.

She stroked my face as I had her stockings on. "Mummy...". She muttered.

My eyes started to cry. I embraced her.

"Mama, remain with Daddy." She muttered.

She said something that surprised me.

I carried her in my arms to the waiting school bus.

After Kate's school bus had left, Katie was assisting John in tying his tie when I arrived at the home.

Such a beautiful scene.

It stung to witness another lady touch a guy who had previously been my husband's collar.

They were in a compromising position, so I attempted to disguise the gurgling, sickening sensation that was developing inside of me and cleared my throat so they would see me. My eyes met John's.

"I'm heading to work. I'll go there and pick up Kate from school. I pronounced it as formally as I could.

I'll drop you off, please. I saw Katie's dissatisfied expression as he approached me. I shrugged and walked after him as I saw him leave the home. John and I hadn't sat in his vehicle together in a while.

His tie was not correctly tied.

I made him forget how to knot ties since I was the one who always tied his ties.

Could I assist you with that?

He was taken aback by my unexpected suggestion.

I was aware it would bring back memories of when we were first married when I used to tie his tie every morning before he left for work and then stopped doing it for him once I became busy at work.

As I correctly tied his tie, I could hear his heartbeat.

"I'm grateful," When I finished tying his tie, he mumbled and belted his seatbelt.

As I fastened my seatbelt, I saw him start the vehicle.

He turned to face me as he continued down the road. What are your plans for Coker Lee?

"Even if I wanted to inspire optimism in any guy, now is not the time. That would be disrespectful of me. In addition, I struggle to adore a guy whose affection grows as a result of rivalry.

What type of a guy are you looking for to love?" He said it while gazing out the window of the automobile. How do I tell him that he was the sort of guy I was looking for?

John was so unusual. How much I wish he could comprehend.

I sighed. Just a guy who won't abandon me the way you did. You abandoned me. A different guy from you is who I desire. A guy who will not abandon me. This time, it was my turn to avert his gaze.

He kept quiet.

till we arrived at my workplace.

When I exited his vehicle and started to leave, he waved at me.

His expression indicated that he was already regretting our rash decision to file for divorce.

Me too.

Can we please return to the good old days where we never fought?

My telephone rang.

I plugged the line in.

Hello, ma?" Are you Martin kate's mother? Your daughter was one of the students our driver transported this morning on the school bus. She unfortunately also got into a collision. Please get in touch with your spouse and get straight to Gateprince Hospital.

Due to my emotions, I was unable to drive to the location, so I waited patiently for John to show up.

The John I knew was in him.

John could maintain self-control under pressure. He hugged me even though I was shaking and crying. It worked, that hug. It gave my fluttering heart solace.

While moving forward, he let go of me but kept his left hand in mine.

How in the world did I imagine that I would survive without this man?

A guy, he was.

A true lady also needs a real guy.

We stopped in the automobile when we arrived at the hospital.

Never before in my life have I felt this terrified.

He was the first person to get out of the vehicle and assist me.

We walked to the hospital after he had secured the vehicle.

The emergency unit already had Kate inside.

I wept hysterically.

I asked God to take my life rather than the life of my daughter.

My poor kid, who was too little to experience parental separation and is still in such anguish.

We waited patiently for the doctor as I laid my head on his shoulder. We didn't get to witness our child's serious condition, so we followed him to his office.

"I only hope her brain wasn't damaged as a result of the head injuries. Because if it did, one of these negative news stories would exist. The first is that she may not make it or could awaken retarded.

I yelled. "How is this possible! Where is that idiot driver? I growled and stood to my feet.

The driver passed away barely two minutes ago. The physician stated.

It had been such a horrific accident.

"Doctor, may I simply stand back and observe my child? Please, I simply want to see my kid, no matter the distance.

It is not a beautiful sight.

I pushed through the nurse attempting to stop me as I left his office and hurried to meet my kid.

At the sight of my kid, I shook.

My kid was gone from my sight.

I was aware of the excruciating agony.

Kate wasn't strong enough to handle such suffering.

Why did I have to enter this planet to cause my kid suffering?

I stumbled over to John's automobile.

He was seated in the vehicle.

Weeping...

John was in tears.

John never before had I seen him cry.

Because of the manner, he was crying, it hurt more.

I feigned not to see him crying, and when he realized I was there, he hastily dabbed away his tears and watched me get into the vehicle.

"Gloria, stay with me tonight." He hugged me. "I don't believe I am in a good enough frame of mind to be left alone."

"How is Katie doing?"

After releasing me, he looked into my eyes. "Katie is not the mother of kate."

I wanted to remain with him as well.

I blinked. Since you are Kate's father, I shall accede to your request.

He took a car to his large home.

Katie hurried out of the home as soon as we entered. She had a spatula in her hand. Cooking must be something. "How's Kate doing?"

We don't want to discuss it, Katie. We want solitude. John spoke sternly to her.

"We???". The woman was shocked.

"You still don't have a conscience! Both parents are weeping for their kid." We went inside his room as he growled at her.

a big room.

larger than the one in our previous residence.

He undid his tie. "I gathered my belongings and left that place because I didn't want anything to make me think of you. You are now in my room. The irony of life

I gave a meaningful nod before sitting on the bed.

He positioned his arm around me as he sat next to me. The entrance was opened.

With a dish of soup and yam, Katie entered.

She reluctantly handed John the food tJohn. When is Benedicta going so she may return home and recover, John?

"Benedicta will reside here while kate is recovering,"

She can relax at her folks' house, John! At him, Katie shot.

"I need her assistance!" But the health of Kate is at stake! How is having her at your side going to be of any use? I don't have to explain to you who I want living here, and if you don't like them, you may leave. "Kate is the sole reason I am still here. I'll hold off till she gets well. She stomped out of the room. "Where am I going to bed tonight?" Curious, I questioned him.

Where are you going to sleep?

"Yes"

"You are welcome to use the bed. I'll use the duvet to sleep.

Once again, I was a virgin.

I blocked out all the nights and mornings we spent making love in the past.

I had to appear as if nothing had ever occurred between us since, in my eyes, I had never slept with John in my life and he had never been my husband.

I took my clothes off in the dressing room and wrapped his enormous towel over my body before going directly to the bathroom to have a shower.

As soon as I left, John hurried in to replace me.

We had finished having a bath.

He slept on the duvet as I dozed on the bed.

The large room was silent, yet we were both awake.

After deciding to speak, Johnmond rubbed his throat. How did things turn out between us? "Why did we split up?"

"For marriage, I neglected to fulfill my responsibilities as a wife and mother."

"How about me? What was wrong with me?

I gulped as I made an effort to consider his failing. "You acted on impulse a lot."

Do you believe so?

"I am aware."

"Did our imperfections sever our love for one another?"

"Er...

I am unaware of that. I was unable to speak the truth due to my pride.

Do you believe that I can lose all interest in you?

Why not?" You got rid of me!

Where is the evidence that I divorced you, you ask?

I didn't understand what he was saying. "Proof? How?".

"You were the one who was hasty, therefore you divorced without evidence,"

"John, you're confounding me."

My telephone rang. Coker Lee was there.

I made it work. "Hello".

"I was aware of your daughter. I'm really sad about your loss.

I yelled at the telephone. "Loss? My daughter is still alive!

Yes, I am aware. But Benedicta , 98 percent of those students had already passed away.

"Never use this number again." I glared back at him.

"I moved your daughter to the VIP unit already." He spoke.

At the sound of it, my heart sank. "What did you do?"

"Your daughter is the person in the world who means most to you. I am aware of all of that, and my greatest desire is to preserve your delight.

Many thanks, Coker Lee.

"Don't bring it up at all."

"Are you available tomorrow?"

"Where are you at this moment?"

"At home or the home of your ex-husband?"

For the time being, I wish to sleep in my daughter's room.

"I perceive. But be careful not to approach that guy too closely.

John snuggled me as soon as he spoke that phrase, getting into bed next to me.

I cut the connection and, astonished, turned to face him. What are you doing, John?

"I dare the guy attempting to win your heart for financial gain. I want to show you both that I wasn't sleeping on the duvet earlier because I was afraid of being near to you, but rather because I wanted to make you feel comfortable.

"John, we're divorced."

"Who was the attorney responsible?"

The decision is yours. My divorce papers were given to me by you.

I shouldn't be able to touch the mother of my kid whether I've given you divorce papers or not, she said.

"However, just because you are the mother of my kid doesn't mean you can touch me."

"...and I'll say it once more. Both of my decisions to distance myself from you and to come closer to you were made consciously.

The next morning I was awake before anybody else in the house and hurried enthusiastically to clean.

I was radiating too many uplifting feelings.

In the first place, I had a maternal feeling that my daughter would live, and in the second place, John had snuggled me the whole night.

Even after our marriage, I still longed for his cuddles.

We stopped having regular sex and hugs after three years of marriage.

We merely had sex now, no longer made love.

We stopped consciously touching one other and started doing so simply because of hormones.

We had been making love for three years, but eventually, it simply turned into sex, which we still indulged in sometimes.

Why did I still want my ex-husband even after he had hugged me the night before?

Why were his arms still so cozy and warm?

Why was I still secretly holding onto the notion that he was still mine?

Why did I still care so much for him?

As I cleaned the large home, I enthusiastically hummed.

His filthy clothes were heaped up in the basket, I saw.

Then I dried and cleaned them.

I made rice and veggie soup.

I heard footsteps coming from behind as I was gathering everyone in the kitchen to start cooking.

Katie appeared.

She gave me a look. "Why did you cook and clean the house? That is what I do.

Why do you do it for a living?

I find this question to be foolish.

"Stupid inquiry? Probably because I'm speaking to an idiot, my inquiry seems foolish.

John entered just as she raised her fist to strike me.

He felt astounded. What did you want to accomplish? Why would you hit a mom who is still in mourning over the terrible health of her child?

"Does she seem to be mourning at the moment?"

After leaving the kitchen, he came back seven minutes later. "Katie, I have your belongings organized in my second vehicle.

I'll take them immediately away in my car to your place.

"John, are you removing me from this residence because of her?"

"I don't want you here, therefore I'm removing you from this home. I hope you won't be here, Katie. At all".

But do you want her present?

I get to make that decision. He went outside.

He came back a few minutes later with a serious expression. How come you cleaned the house?

I sighed. "I just felt like it."

Do you think I pushed for a divorce because I had too many chores? Simply put, it was due to a lack of communication between us. Recognizing when we're both worn out. Recognizing when we're both attempting to put things right. There is no difference between whether you clean or not.

"You were the home head; I was supposed to be the home manager. Your role was to supervise, and mine was to put things right. John, it's been a while since I prepared food for you. I missed preparing food for you.

He was looking at me with tears in his eyes. I was missing your meals.

My telephone rang.

a strange number.

I made it work. "Hello?".

Your kid has opened her eyes. Your daughter has a chance of living. Not even retarded, she is. She has survived.

Chapter 5

"Papa, mama." When she opened her eyes, she whispered.

We embraced her. I gave her cornflakes to eat till she was full before lulling her to sleep with a song. The doctor urged us to leave the ward after she had slept off so that she could have a decent rest.

I was happy. Though she still had bruises all over her body, my only kid was improving, and it is a marvel that she can open her eyes and even eat.

Coker Lee was standing nearby. How is she doing?

Very substantially improved. I appreciate you moving her to the VIP ward. I was grateful to him.

He gave John a sly smirk. "I accomplished for you what your ex-husband was unable to. He was unable to improve your daughter's condition.

I was surprised to hear John laugh. "In terms of my daughter's life, I applaud everyone who helped her."

I could see that Coker Lee was as astounded by John's answer as I was.

My parents and John's parents both appeared at once.

I was taken aback to see them there, particularly my parents, whom I had never informed about my child's illness out of concern for their safety.

They gave me a dirty look.

They were upset with me.

How is Kate currently? My mom questioned John.

She had access to food and sleep. She is improving.

Her mother John grunted. "We have determined that you two will remain husband and wife as soon as Kate is released from the hospital."

"Wife and husband?" John and I both sobbed.

"Yes". My dad responded. "Playing with a four-year- old is not appropriate. The kid needs both parents to be together, especially at this period.

Before the kid may enjoy them, they do not need to be married. Lee Coker proposed.

Our parents just realized he had been standing there at that point.

Who are you, I ask. John's dad inquired of him.

"My name is Coker Lee, and I'm a celebrity. It was thanks to me that your daughter's health improved when I moved her to the VIP unit. I took those actions because I think of Kate as my daughter. Benedicta does not have to be John's bride.

"You may go, thank you." My dad growled at him.

He left furiously.

John and I ate on the balcony while I made rice and beans.

His telephone rang.

He put the phone number on the loudspeaker since it was unknown. Why did you and your wife fake a divorce? I answered the phone and heard the caller's voice.

Lee Coker.

Phony divorce? How???

He handed the phone to me, and I quickly put it in my ear. "Coker, what do you mean by a phony divorce?"

"Since no attorney was present when you made that dumb signature on a blank piece of paper, it seems that you and John are still married. Despite Johnson, you are still Benedicta Martin.

I was astounded by what he told me, and John's reaction at that very time proved that he was correct.

I cut the connection and turned to face John. "John?".

"I lacked the confidence to end our relationship altogether. It was all I could do to separate. How do you think I'm going to end our marriage forever? How certain was I that we would return? But not forever, I simply wanted some distance from you. And Benedicta , that's plenty of room. The fact that you are still my wife won't ever change.

His phone rang once more.

And the caller was the same.

The line was connected, and the speakers were turned on.

Hello, please check WhatsApp. The line was cut off by him.

He opened the WhatsApp program, and we both saw the messages that Coker Lee had sent to him.

It was a video of our daughter being wheeled out of the ward she was being held in.

We both panicked, and John instantly phoned the number.

"Last night, your parents told me face-to-face that you two can only reunite if your daughter wakes up. Your parents are currently unaware that the divorce was a fraud. You are aware of the consequences of your daughter's medicine is delayed for two days, correct? I'll allow you two days to consult with a divorce lawyer and file the necessary paperwork. There is a 100% probability that you won't see your only kid again if that happens. The line was cut off by him.

All through the night, I was the only one who was frightened. John remained silent.

He didn't do anything except sit next to me on the bed and stroke his bottom lip. "John, the situation of our daughter is serious. If we even slightly postpone giving her her meds. His telephone rang. Coker Lee had previously called him at the same number. As John made the connection, I saw him grinning mischievously.

"What the hell did you do, you bastard!" Lee Coker growled.

I was perplexed. What had Johnmond done to provoke such rage in Coker Lee?

Throat-clearing by Johnmond The public will learn how much money your father stole before he quit last month when the enormous sum is handed to them in two hours.

"Do you believe that threatens me?"

You have always defended your father's reputation more than your own from the beginning. I am aware of your strong preference for your father's reputation above your own life. Call me when you're ready. The line was cut off by him.

John, how did you manage to withdraw such a large sum of money from his father's account?

"The kid of his father's best buddy is my spy. We attended the same secondary institution. I'm going to accomplish two goals at once. I have the authority and the proof necessary to detain Coker Lee and return my daughter.

How will you carry it out?

"Just keep an eye out."

I started to appreciate him more after that.

One hour after Coker Lee and John's conversation, my daughter was left in front of the hospital, and the physicians hurried out to carry her to the hospital on a stretcher.

The next morning, John and I hurried to the hospital to visit my kid, and when we got there, we saw that she was even more cheerful than she had been the day before.

Coker Lee arrived in the ward where she was being held to greet us. As soon as I started to scowl at him, he dropped to his knees. He looked at John. "Even if you have evidence, why didn't you pursue the case against me?"

You are a pathetic person, that's why. stated John.

Coker Lee wept. "Up to the very end, you were superior to me. till the very end.

"Coker, why don't you put the past behind you? Why? I am not trying to replace you. We are now guys. You need to open your eyes to see it.

"You had a gorgeous daughter and the nicest wife. You don't have the same level of financial stability that I have, but you are pleased. My whole life has been spent attempting to make up for something that was not your fault. I wanted to attack you, therefore I wanted to get your wife. I did not live for myself but you.

Coker, go out there and start enjoying your life for yourself right now.

How do I carry it out? I have grown older.

'You can do that. Years are yet ahead of you. He was helped up to his feet.

Coker Lee looked across to me. "I apologize for everything. I hope you now see the real worth of family and how pointless life would be without it. Never, not even for fame, let go of your family. After realizing everything we have accomplished in life, we look back and see that family was our priority and will always be our top priority even after everything else. He gave John a shoulder pat before leaving the ward.

I was moved by what had transpired, and I was pleased that Coker Lee was able to go back and follow his path.

I embraced John.

"Mama, dada." When we overheard Kate murmur, we broke apart, turned to face her, and sat next to her on the sick bed. She was smiling at us while sitting up.

We hurried to embrace her. She was healing so quickly. It was clear that Coker Lee's doctor had handled her flawlessly the previous evening. Even her bruise was recovering quite quickly. Undoubtedly a pricey procedure.

John glanced up at me after we had hugged our daughter and noted that she would soon be heading home with us. Are you prepared to rejoin me as my wife, Benedicta ? Are you prepared to live with me once again, this time for all eternity?

Chapter 6

Even two weeks after my kid was released from the hospital and I had no firm answer for John.

In John's lovely chamber, she had, at last, managed to get some rest.

She had slept off thanks to the white soup I had made especially for her and given her that morning.

John was at the door when I realized he was thereafter covering and setting his supper on the dining room table.

Before I could leave the home, he closed the door and started to come near me. "You promised to respond to my question when Kate gets released from the hospital. Today, Kate made a return. was taken aback by his actions and told him, "You won't leave until you give me your answer.

In actuality, I was terrified to return to my house.

What if I ultimately make another mistake, causing us to part ways once more?

Was I certain that I would be able to fulfill John's desire for a decent wife in his life?

John looked into my eyes. "I am aware of your thoughts. You are worried that you could fall short of the requirements I have for a bride. Benedicta , I appreciate all of your work. I'm aware that I hardly deserve someone like you. But if you leave me, I have no idea what I'll do.

I cried. "John, I became quite afraid about losing my family when I saw that weird lady with you. That's when I realized how terrified I was of losing you. I'm not sure I could survive without you.

Before I knew it, John had me in his arm and was giving me his trademark kiss.

...like he was in control of my body and looking for the love on my lips.

As he caressed me, tears started to fall down my face.

I missed my hubby.

My body, soul, and spirit.

He had made love to me for the first time in a long time and held me all night.

Even though we had been having sex for a very long time, the way his touch made my body feel made me realize that having sex with your spouse is not the same as making love with him.

Every contact was deliberate.

"I've already sent my lads to box everything up and bring it back here to where it belongs from your parents' home," I said.

I shrieked. "So quickly?"

He laughed. "I was worried that if you went back home to grab your stuff on your own, you may change your mind and decide not to come back to me."

I chuckled. You bother me so much.

"I miss you," He said softly into my ear as he watched me laugh. What work-related plans do you have?

"My employer phoned me yesterday as a married lady for the first time. There was a period when I had the idea that once my employer saw the effects of my marriage on me, he would get discouraged and think he should have hired a single person rather than a married lady like me. But I've come to realize that I haven't given my job and marriage the ideal amount of time and that by giving workers more time, I have made a lot of errors. But I want to be a good wife and mother first.

He kissed me on the forehead. "I'll make an effort to improve my financial situation for you and my kid. Any misunderstanding between us is an opportunity for us to learn from our errors and better understand one another. You have my undying affection, Benedicta .

"My darling, I adore you too."

As soon as he entered our room, Kate leaped up and down on our bed.

We hugged her close to us.

I have never before in my life seen my daughter seem so content.

My daughter had made it through the accident, and I had returned to my family.

What more could I possibly want?

Now that I know it, a woman who has a successful home is more successful than a woman who has a broken home, even if she has a good career because the actual successful woman is a woman who is successful in both her home and career.

I'm still progressively developing to become the best wife I can be.

for my household.

to myself.

THE END.

www.ingramcontent.com/pod-product-compliance
Lightning Source LLC
Chambersburg PA
CBHW051450150726
48000CB00005B/2338